StoryKits

monday morning®

WHOLE LANGUAGE ACTIVITIES

Patterns to use with
favorite predictable books

by Candy Jones and Lea McGee, illustrated by Marilynn G. Barr

Publisher: Roberta Suid
Editor: Carol Whiteley
Production: Susan Cronin-Paris

Entire contents copyright ©1991 by Monday Morning
Books, Inc., Box 1680, Palo Alto, California 94302

Monday Morning is a registered trademark of
Monday Morning Books, Inc.

ISBN 1-878279-28-9

Printed in the United States of America
9 8 7 6 5 4 3 2 1

For a complete catalog, write to the address above.

Contents

The Very Hungry Caterpillar

The Mitten

Mr. Gumpy's Outing

Introduction

All children have favorite storybooks they love to listen to again and again. StoryKits is designed to help you accompany and extend six time-tested storybook favorites with a variety of drama, cooking, art, writing, and language activities. The activities are appropriate for young children in preschools, kindergartens, child care, after-school programs, and at home.

What Are StoryKits?

Each of the six kits in StoryKits contains materials that focus on helping children explore a well-loved, predictable storybook: The Runaway Bunny, On Market Street, Cat Goes Fiddle-i-fee, The Mitten, The Very Hungry Caterpillar, and Mr. Gumpy's Outing. Because predictable storybooks have repeated words and events, children can join in reading them right away. And because they're easy to remember, children can retell the stories using the familiar story words.

Each storykit provides follow-up activities that relate to the storybook: cooking activities that tie into the story's theme; art projects that focus on the setting or action of the story; bookmaking that involves children in creating their own special stories for sharing and retelling; and the how-to's for story dramatizations using flannel board, clothesline, and pocket props made from reproducible patterns. A list of additional related books and a reproducible pattern for drawing and writing books are also included.

Learning with StoryKits

Reading stories aloud to children has many benefits. It enlivens children's experiences with unfamiliar language, events, and characters. It stimulates emotions and helps children understand other people and places. It also allows children to enter imaginary worlds. Accompanying the reading of favorite storybooks with the StoryKits materials will further enrich children's learning.

Cooking and Art Activities. These activities will help children learn to follow directions while accomplishing a goal. In cooking, math concepts such as counting and measuring will be practiced; through artwork, aesthetic concepts of color, line, texture, and shape will be discovered. As the children talk about their cooking and eating experiences and about creating art, they will be enhancing their language development as well as their vocabulary.

Bookmaking. Retelling, "writing," drawing, and dictating each story will enrich the children's self-esteem and communication skills; the activities will also be valuable preparation for future reading and writing. Remember as the children work that they won't really be writing a story, but their scribble writing will be one way they can learn about writing. The experience of creating a storybook—not the correctness of the result—is what is important for development and learning.

Dramatizations. Using flannel board, clothesline, or pocket props, the children will be able to retell the stories repeatedly, in different dramatizations. This retelling will enrich the children's vocabulary as they incorporate the sophisticated language of the stories. It will also help the children gain a sense of sequence, descriptive language, and cause-effect relationships. The firsthand experiences with stories, authors, and characters will add to the children's later ability to read and write.

Getting Ready

The following steps will help you prepare the StoryKits materials for use.

1. Check out the particular storybook from your local library or purchase it at a bookstore. All the storybooks are currently in print, available in paperback, and reasonably priced.

2. Obtain several books on the kit's Related Books list to help expand awareness of the storybook's central theme.

3. Gather the items needed for the cooking, art, and writing activities you wish to do using the various materials lists.

4. Use the reproducible book pattern and follow the directions for preparing a blank book of lined or unlined paper for each child. The children will be able to help put the books together.

5. Follow the kit's instructions for making the flannel board, clothesline, or pocket props; the children may be able to help.

Clothesline props will require a line and clip-on clothespins; pocket props will be placed in a pocket such as a mitten.

How to Use StoryKits

Begin by reading the storybook aloud to the children. Then read it again the next day using the storytelling props (you will probably want to practice reading the story using the props before you read to the children). Invite the children to add to the story.

Read the story again the following day, and ask the children to manipulate the props as you read. Then read some of the related books aloud. Continue reading the story, working with the props, and reading the related books as long as the children remain interested. Display the storybook and the props to encourage the children to "read" and retell the story on their own (some children may "read" the storybooks by memorizing the texts). Also display the related books for the children to pretend to read.

Each day you read the story or one of the related books, you may want to do a cooking, art, or writing activity. Cooking activities need adult supervision (picture recipes will help younger children), but the children can complete the art activities on their own once the technique has been demonstrated or the directions given. Invite the children to draw or "write" in their blank books or let them dictate stories for you to write down.

The Runaway Bunny

This is a repetitive story about a little bunny who decides to run away from his mother. He tells her he will become a fish, then a rock, a crocus, a bird, a sailboat, a bunny on a flying trapeze, and a little boy to escape her. But his mother tells the little bunny that if he becomes these things, she will follow him each time and find him, because he's her little bunny. The bunny decides he might just as well stay at home. The Runaway Bunny by Margaret Wise Brown (Harper & Row, 1942).

Related Books

The following books focus on mothers' love, travel, and rabbits.

Diary of a Rabbit by Lilo Hess (Scribner's, 1982).

Have You Seen My Duckling? by Nancy Tafuri (Greenwillow, 1984).

Little Fox Goes to the End of the World by Ann Tompert (Crown, 1976).

The Little Rabbit Who Wanted Red Wings by Carolyn Bailey (Putnam, 1931).

Little Rabbit's Loose Tooth by Lucy Bate (Crown, 1975).

Rabbits, Rabbits by Aileen Fisher (Harper & Row, 1983).

The Tale of Peter Rabbit by Beatrix Potter (Warne, 1902).

Three Ducks Went Wandering by Ron Roy (Houghton Mifflin, 1979).

Cooking Activities

Carrot Cookies

2 eggs	1 cup brown sugar
$\frac{2}{3}$ cup cooking oil	$1\frac{3}{4}$ cups all-purpose flour
1 teaspoon baking powder	1 teaspoon cinnamon
$\frac{1}{4}$ teaspoon salt	1 cup shredded carrots
$\frac{3}{4}$ cup raisins	powdered sugar

Preheat the oven to 350 degrees. Beat the eggs, brown sugar, and oil together in a large bowl. Sift together the flour, baking powder, cinnamon, and salt in another bowl. Gradually add the flour mixture to the egg mixture. Stir in the carrots and raisins. Pour the mixture into a greased 15" x 10" x 1" baking pan and bake for 25 minutes. Cool. Sprinkle the top with powdered sugar. Cut into 35 squares.

Bunny Salad

2 apples	$\frac{1}{4}$ cup mayonnaise
2 carrots	$\frac{1}{4}$ cup sour cream
2 celery stalks	$\frac{1}{4}$ teaspoon lemon juice
$\frac{1}{4}$ cup raisins	

Cut the apples into slices. Help the children dice the slices and the celery stalks. Help the children peel and grate the carrots. Then let the children stir the mayonnaise, sour cream, and lemon juice together in a large bowl. Add the apples, carrots, celery, and raisins. Stir. Refrigerate before serving. Makes 10 to 12 portions.

Sailboats

10 eggs	salt
10 slices of cheese	pepper
3 tablespoons mayonnaise	

Cook the eggs in boiling water until hard boiled. Peel the eggs and cut in half lengthwise. Help the children remove the egg yolks. Have the children mix the yolks and the mayonnaise in a small bowl. Add salt and pepper to taste. Help the children spoon the yolk mixture back into the egg halves. Cut each cheese slice into two triangles. Weave each triangle onto a toothpick to make a sail. Have the children stick a cheese sail into the yolk of each egg half to form a sailboat. Makes 20 sailboats.

Art Activities

Bunny Collages

Materials: 18" x 12" sheets of construction paper; collage materials such as fabric scraps, lace, feathers, fancy paper scraps, Styrofoam shapes, and cotton balls; scissors; glue; markers

Preparation: Draw a simple bunny shape and duplicate enough shapes on construction paper to give one to each child. Have each child cut out a shape, or cut the bunnies out for them. Cut the collage materials into small pieces.

Activity: Have the children glue various bits of the materials to their bunnies. They may add facial features with markers.

Bunny Tail Paintings

Materials: cotton balls, powdered tempera paint, construction paper, hair spray, marker, glue, small bowls

Preparation: Draw a large bunny shape on construction paper for each child. Place a different color of paint powder into each of several bowls.

Activity: Let the children dip cotton balls into the different paints and dab, rub, or stroke the color onto the bunnies. When painting is completed, the children may glue their cotton-ball brushes onto the paper to make the bunny's colorful tail. Spray the finished artwork with hair spray to set the paint.

Rock Bunnies

Materials: smooth, 2-inch-diameter rocks; toothbrushes; white tempera paint; water; brushes; black markers

Preparation: Take the children on a walk to gather rocks, or have them bring rocks to class. Let the children clean their rocks with water and a toothbrush. Set the rocks aside to dry.

Activity: Tell the children to paint the rocks with white paint. When the paint is dry, let the children use the markers to draw bunny faces on the rocks.

Storytelling

Bookmaking

Materials: bookmaking patterns, pink and white construction paper, unlined or lined writing paper, ribbon or yarn, scissors, hole punch, glue, markers

Preparation: Duplicate enough bunny body patterns on pink construction paper to give two to each child. Cut the patterns out (let the children do this if they are able). Duplicate the body pattern on writing paper (use the dotted line as a guide), cut out, and give three or four sheets to each child. Duplicate the bunny arm patterns on white construction paper, cut out, and give two to each child.

Activity: Have the children glue a bunny arm to each side of one of their bunny shapes; this will be the front of the book. Let the children use markers to add features to the bunny. Then help the children put the writing paper shapes between the front cover and the other construction paper bunny. Punch two holes at the top of each bunny book as indicated on the pattern. Thread ribbon or yarn through the holes and tie in a bow. Let the children use their bunny books for writing, drawing, or dictating. (See the completed book on the first page of this kit.)

Flannel Board Storytelling

Materials: storytelling patterns, large flannel board, assorted colors of flannel (props can also be made from construction paper patterns or colored reproducible patterns with Velcro glued to the back), scissors, glue, markers

Preparation: Cut out the patterns and trace each onto a piece of the appropriate color of flannel. Cut out the flannel shapes and add details with markers. Using the illustrations in The Runaway Bunny as a guide, put the patterns in order for storytelling.

Activity: As you read or retell the story, put up the patterns in the order they are mentioned. For some you will add the mother or the baby bunny to another pattern, for example, place the mother on the tightrope. If you wish, let a child or several children put the patterns on the board. Later, have the children retell the story and put up the patterns as they speak. Also encourage the children to use their imaginations to think of other ways the mother could follow her baby bunny.

Bookmaking Patterns

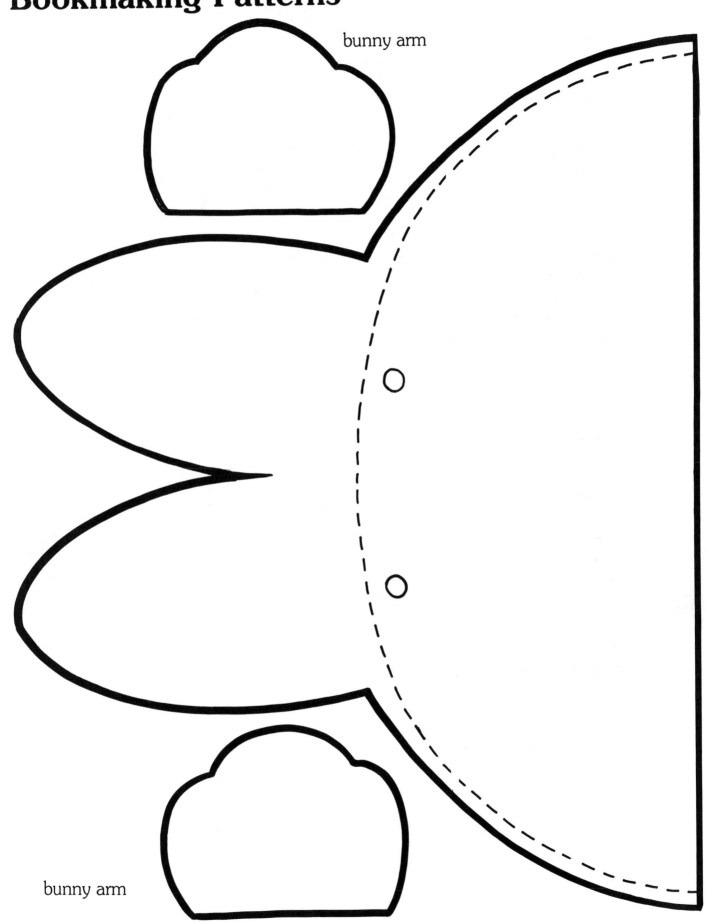

bunny arm

bunny arm

Bookmaking Pattern

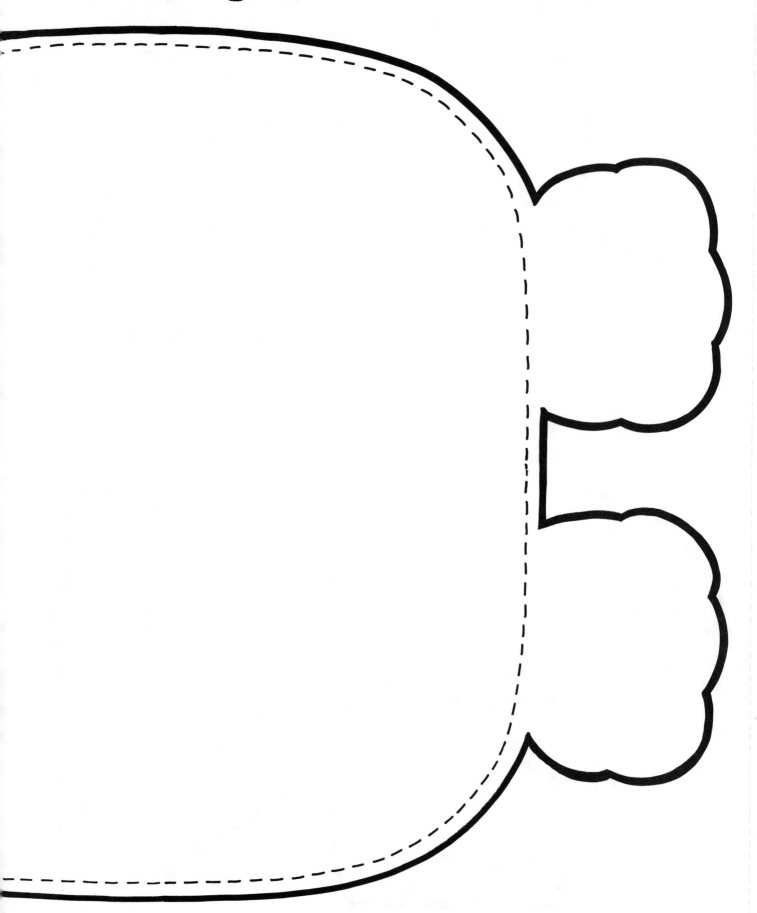

Storytelling Patterns

mother's fishing rod

net

mother

bunny

bunny's stream

bunny's rock

Storytelling Patterns

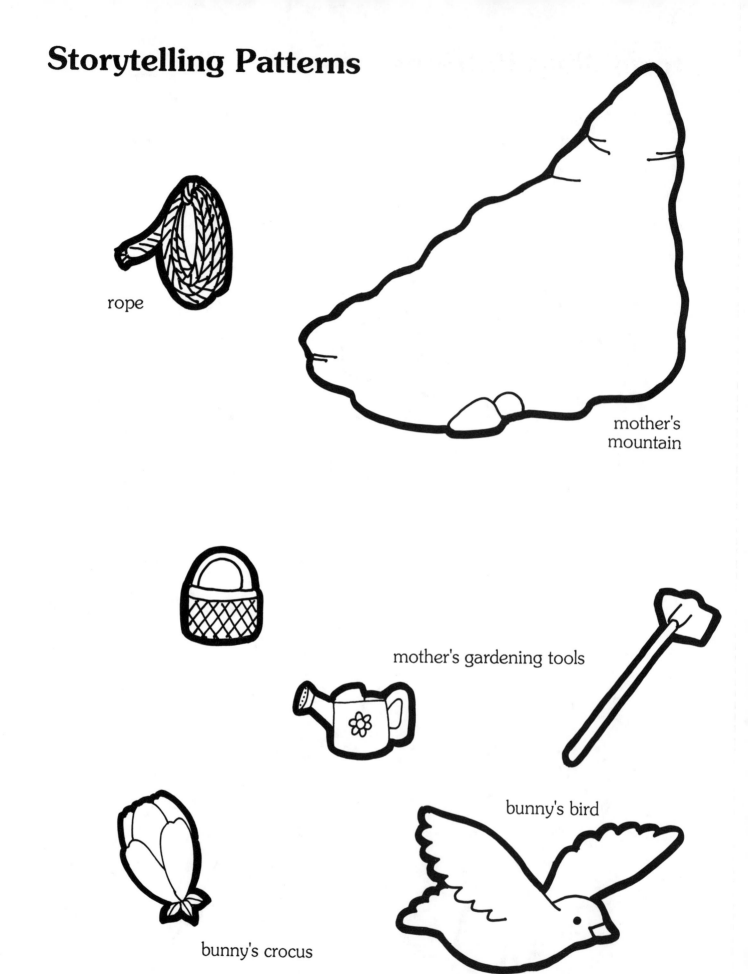

rope

mother's mountain

mother's gardening tools

bunny's bird

bunny's crocus

Storytelling Patterns

bunny's sailboat

mother's wind

mother's tree

Storytelling Patterns

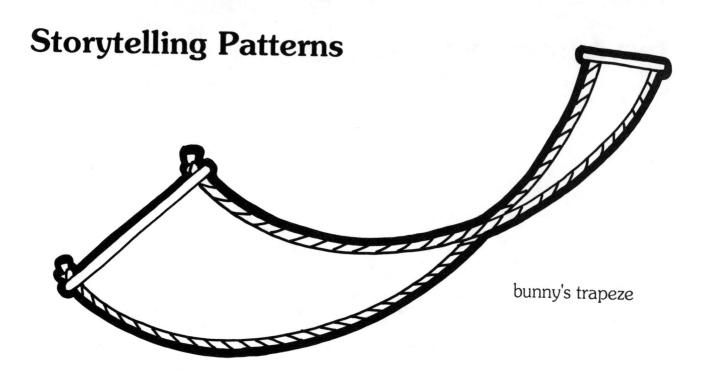

bunny's trapeze

mother's umbrella

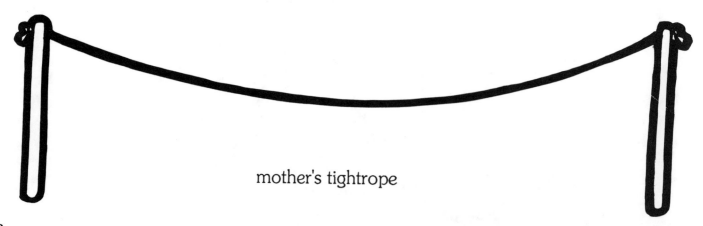

mother's tightrope

16

On Market Street

This is a predictable story about a boy who strolls down Market Street buying gifts for a friend. The merchants on Market Street offer a wide array of merchandise, each item starting with one of the letters of the alphabet. Each item is beautifully illustrated in the book with the items arranged in the shape of a person. On Market Street by Arnold Lobel (Greenwillow, 1981).

Related Books

The following books focus on the alphabet, cities, markets, and shopping.

Amazing Animal Alphabet Book by Roger and Mariko Chouinard (Doubleday, 1988).

Animal Alphabet by Bert Kitchen (Dial, 1984).

Anno's Flea Market by Mitsumasa Anno (Philomel, 1984).

Aster Aardvark's Alphabet Adventure by Steven Kellogg (Morrow, 1987).

General Store by Rachel Field (Greenwillow, 1988).

Museum of Fine Arts, Boston, ABC by Florence Cassen Mayers (Abrams, 1986).

The Story of a Main Street by John S. Goodall (McElderry, 1987).

Supermarket by Anne and Harlow Rockwell (Macmillan, 1979).

Wake Up, City by Alvin Tresselt (Lothrop, 1990).

Cooking Activities

ABC Pretzels

1 package dry yeast

3+ cups flour

$\frac{1}{2}$ cup cold water

1 teaspoon sugar

1 teaspoon salt

Dissolve the yeast in the water. Stir three cups of flour and the sugar together in a large bowl. Add the yeast mixture. Add more flour if necessary, until the mixture holds together. Knead 5 to 10 minutes on a floured surface, then roll into long, thin strands. Have the children shape the strands into alphabet letters. Sprinkle the letters with salt. Bake at 350 degrees for approximately 20 minutes. Makes about 20 letters.

Gelatin Block Letters

4 envelopes unflavored gelatin

3 3-ounce packages flavored gelatin

4 cups boiling water

Combine all the gelatin in a large bowl. Add the water and stir until the gelatin dissolves. Pour the mixture into a 15" x 10" x 1" pan. Chill until set. Use alphabet letter cookie cutters to cut the gelatin. Remove carefully. Makes 18-20 letters.

ABC Snacks

Put out a variety of the following or similar snacks, served in small amounts:

A—apples, apricots

B—bananas, blueberries

C—carrots, cantaloupes

D—dip (for vegetables)

E—eggs, eggplants

F—figs, fruit freezes

G—grapes, grapefruits

H—honeydew melons

I—ice cream

J—juice, jello

K—kiwis, kohlrabi

L—lemonade

M—marshmallows

N—nectarines, navel oranges

O—olives

P—peanuts, pretzels

Q—Quik chocolate mix (with milk)

R—raisins

S—strawberries, scones

T—tangerines, tomatoes

U—Upside Down cake

V—vegetables

W—watermelon, wax beans

Y—yogurt

Z—zucchini

Art Activities

ABC Bleaching

Materials: alphabet cookie cutters, liquid chlorine bleach, colored tissue paper, shallow pan, smocks

Preparation: Pour the bleach into the pan. Have the children put on smocks.

Activity: Have the children gently dip the edges of the cookie cutters into the bleach and stamp them on pieces of tissue paper.

Letter Collages

Materials: newspapers, magazines, glue, scissors, construction paper

Activity: Distribute the magazines, newspapers, and scissors. Have the children cut out letters and glue them to construction paper. The children may choose to cut out only one or two letters—perhaps their initials—or find one of each letter.

Storytelling

Bookmaking

Materials: bookmaking pattern, tagboard, wrapping paper, ribbon, lined or unlined writing paper, scissors, glue, stapler

Preparation: Duplicate enough patterns on tagboard to give two to each child. Cut the patterns out, or have the children do the cutting if they are able. Duplicate and cut out enough patterns from wrapping paper so that each child can have two. Duplicate and cut out enough patterns from writing paper (use the dotted line as a guide) so that each child can have three or four. Cut the ribbon into strips; each child should get one ribbon the length of the tagboard, one ribbon the width of the tagboard, and another long enough to tie into a bow. Tie all the bows.

Activity: Have the children glue each wrapping paper pattern to a tagboard pattern. Then have them glue ribbon across the length and width of one of the wrapping paper-covered patterns (the front) to make it into a present (see the pattern). Have the children glue on the ribbon bow. Show the children how to assemble the front and back tagboard covers with the writing paper in between. Staple along the left side. Encourage the children to use their books for writing, drawing, or dictating.

Another way the children can use their books is to make them into collage books. Have the children cut out pictures of things that can be bought in markets. Then let them work together to paste the pictures into their books, putting all the pictures that begin with A into one book, all those beginning with B in another book, and so on. Place the books in the classroom library for all to share.

Clothesline Storytelling

Materials: storytelling patterns, markers, construction paper, clear Contact paper or laminating film, 12-foot clothesline, two chairs, spring-type clothespins, scissors, glue, basket

Preparation: Color the storytelling patterns with markers and cut them out (either separately or with the letter and its illustration as one unit). Glue each pattern on construction paper. Cut around each pattern, leaving a $\frac{1}{2}$-inch border. Cover with clear Contact paper or laminating film. Put a number of clothespins in the basket.

Activity: Tie the clothesline between two chairs. Put the patterns in order alphabetically. As you read or retell the story, clip each letter pattern and its illustration to the clothesline as mentioned. Later, let the children clip on the letters as they retell the story.

Bookmaking Pattern

Storytelling Patterns

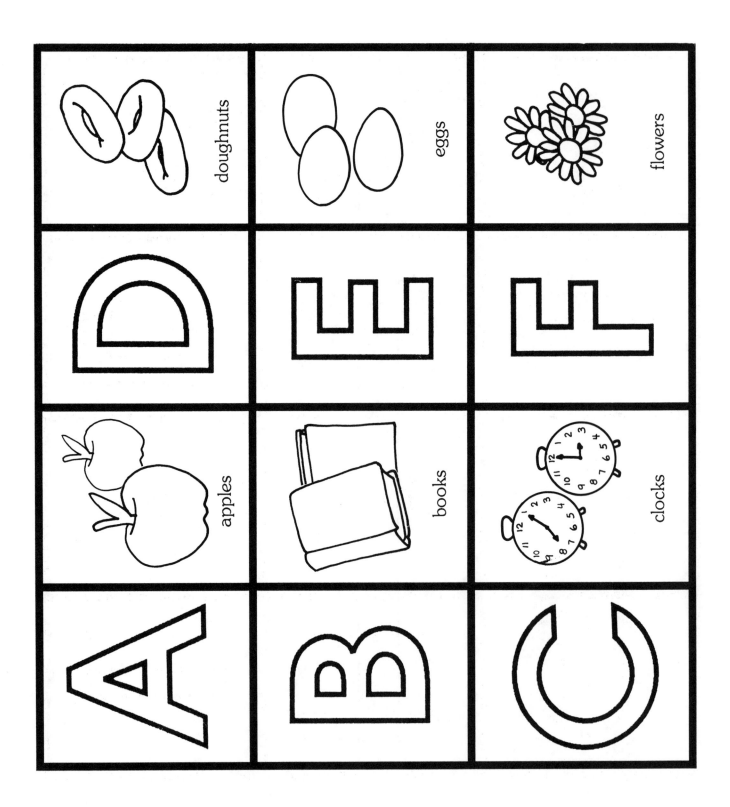

doughnuts

eggs

flowers

apples

books

clocks

Storytelling Patterns

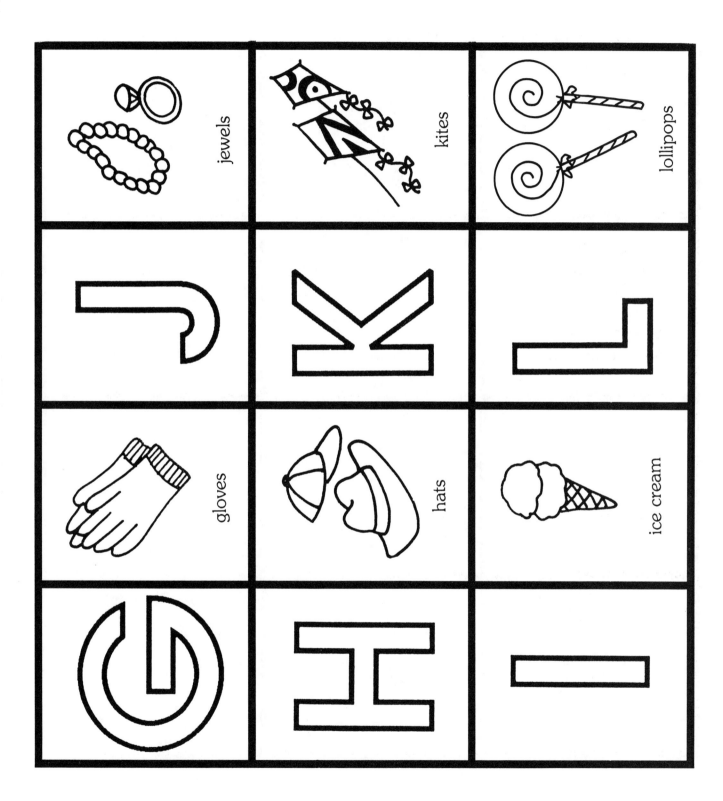

Storytelling Patterns

playing cards

quilts

ribbons

P

Q

R

musical instruments

noodles

oranges

M

N

O

Storytelling Patterns

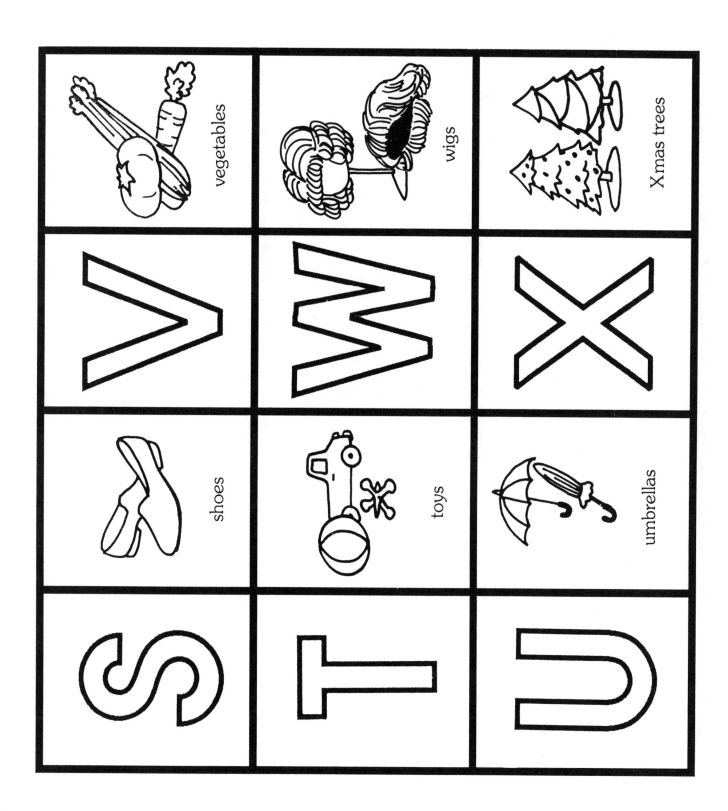

Storytelling Patterns

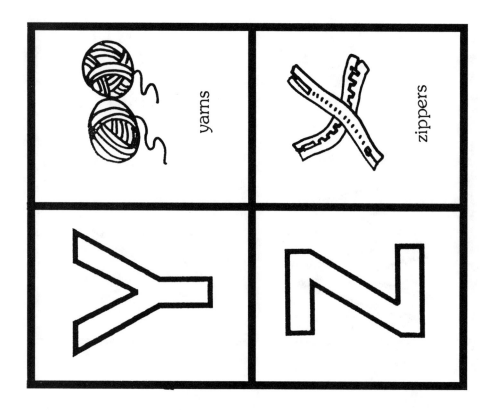

yarns

zippers

Cat Goes Fiddle-i-fee

In this repetitive tale, a little boy feeds a series of farm animals under a big tree. Each animal makes a sound in a cumulative refrain. Finally, the boy's grandmother feeds him. The story ends when everyone takes a nap. <u>Cat Goes Fiddle-i-fee</u> by Paul Galdone (Clarion, 1985).

Related Books

The following stories focus on animals and farm life.

<u>Alligator Arrived with Apples: A Potluck Alphabet Feast</u> by Crescent Dragonwagon (Macmillan, 1987).

<u>Animal Alphabet</u> by Bert Kitchen (Dial, 1984).

<u>Animal Mothers</u> by Atsushi Komori (Putnam, 1983).

<u>AnimAlphabet Encyclopedia</u> by Keith McConnell (Stemmer House, 1982).

<u>Cat</u> by Sara Stein (Harcourt, 1985).

<u>A Cat's Body</u> by Joanna Cole (Morrow, 1982).

<u>A Children's Zoo</u> by Tana Hoban (Greenwillow, 1985).

<u>Early Morning in the Barn</u> by Nancy Tafuri (Greenwillow, 1983).

<u>A Farmer's Alphabet</u> by Mary Azarian (David R. Godine, 1981).

<u>Gobble, Growl, Grunt</u> by Peter Spier (Doubleday, 1971).

<u>Guess What?</u> by Beau Gardner (Lothrop, 1985).

<u>Old MacDonald Had a Farm</u> by Tracey Pearson (Dial, 1986).

Cooking Activities

Grandma's Feed

$\frac{1}{2}$ cup seedless raisins

$\frac{1}{2}$ cup each Wheat Chex,
Rice Chex, Bran Chex

$\frac{1}{2}$ cup Cheerios

$\frac{1}{4}$ cup peanuts or sunflower seeds

Place all the ingredients in a large bowl and stir. Have each child scoop some of the mixture into a plastic bag for snacking. Or let older children follow a picture recipe to mix individual portions in bowls. The recipe makes enough "feed" for six to eight children.

Straw and Hay

4 ounces white linguine

4 ounces green linguine

$\frac{1}{2}$ cup butter or margarine

Parmesan cheese

Cook both types of linguine in boiling, salted water until soft. Drain. Stir in the butter and sprinkle with cheese. Serves 10 to 12 children.

Brown Cows

2 liters root beer

$\frac{1}{2}$ gallon vanilla ice cream

Place one scoop of ice cream into each of 20 large glasses. Pour the root beer over the ice cream. Serve with straws and long spoons.

Art Activities

Animal Stencils

Materials: cardboard or heavyweight paper, pencil or marker, scissors, animal storytelling patterns, manila paper, tempera paint, brushes

Preparation: Make the stencils by tracing each animal pattern onto several pieces of cardboard or stiff paper. Cut the center shapes out.

Activity: Have each child paint a tree on a piece of manila paper. Then have the children stencil animals around the tree.

Feed Baskets

Materials: brown construction paper or paper bags, seeds, rice, popcorn, pasta shells or twists, glue, scissors

Preparation: If children's scissor skills are not strong, cut out enough basket shapes from the brown paper to give one to each child.

Activity: Have the children glue a variety of seeds, pasta, popcorn, and rice to their baskets.

Animal Rubbings

Materials: 5" x 7" pieces of poster board, glue, brushes, animal storytelling patterns, manila paper, crayons, pencil or marker

Preparation: Trace each pattern onto a piece of poster board. Outline each shape with glue. Let dry.

Activity: Give each child a piece of manila paper. Then have each child hold the paper over one of the pieces of poster board and color over the outlined shape. The animal will emerge as a white outline in the colored drawing.

Storytelling

Bookmaking

Materials: bookmaking patterns, green construction paper, brown construction paper, lined or unlined writing paper, glue, stapler, scissors

Preparation: Cut two treetops for each child from the green construction paper; cut along the solid line on the reproducible pattern. Cut two tree trunks for each child from the brown construction paper. Have the children glue each trunk to a treetop. Cut several pieces of paper for each child in the shape of the treetop, cutting along the dotted line on the reproducible pattern.

Activity: Have the children assemble the tree-shaped books by using one tree as the front cover and one tree as the back cover, enclosing several pieces of paper. Staple the books together. Have the children use the books for writing or drawing. (See the completed book on the first page of this kit.)

Flannel Board Storytelling

Materials: storytelling patterns, large flannel board, assorted colors of flannel (props can also be made from construction paper patterns or colored reproducible patterns with Velcro glued to the back), scissors, fine-tipped markers, yarn, fabric scraps, lace, buttons

Preparation: Cut out the patterns and trace each onto a piece of the appropriate color of flannel. Cut out the flannel shapes and add details with the markers. Add other details on the boy and the grandmother such as hair or clothes with yarn, fabric pieces, buttons, and so on.

Activity: Begin by placing the tree and the fence on the flannel board. As you read or tell the story, place each flannel animal and the boy and the grandmother on the board at the appropriate time. Since the story is a cumulative tale, leave the props on the board so that they're all there at the end of the story. After the story has been told and retold, you may want to extend the activity by having the children add other farm animals, and perhaps their voices, to the story.

Bookmaking and Storytelling Patterns

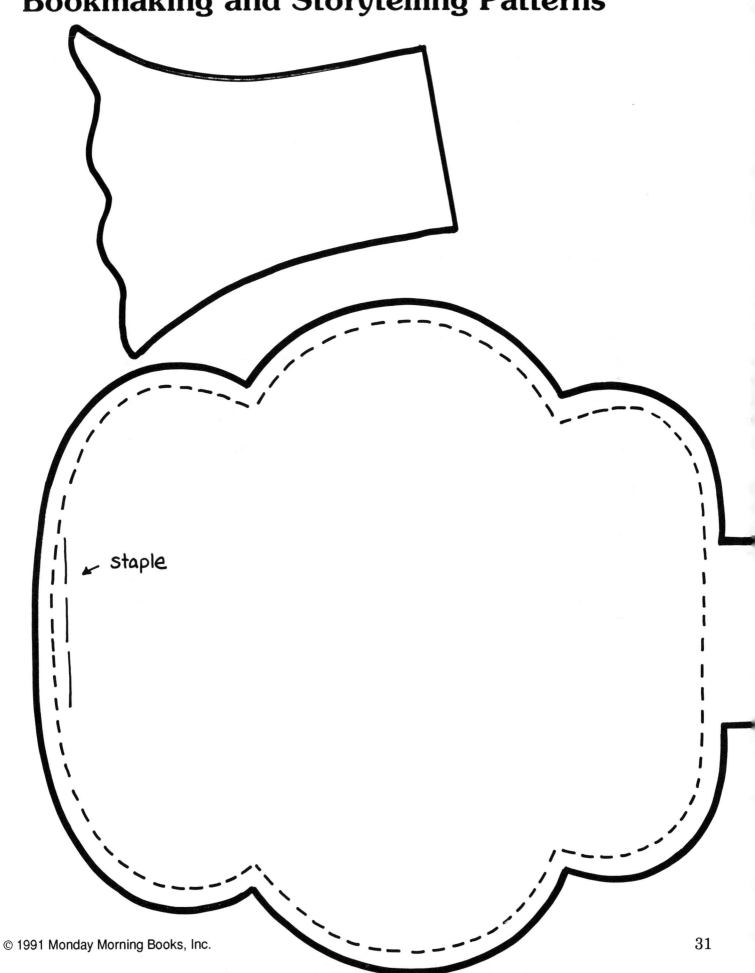

staple

Storytelling Pattern

fence

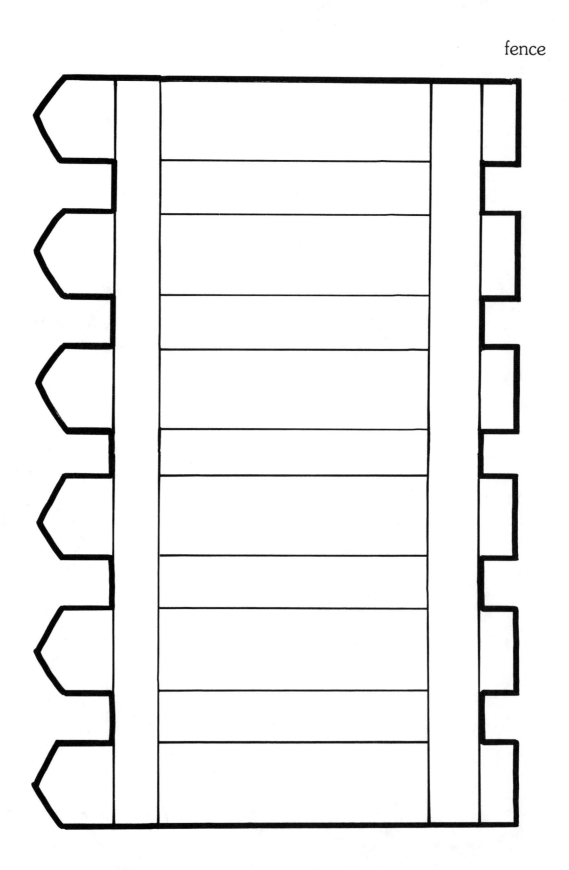

Storytelling Patterns

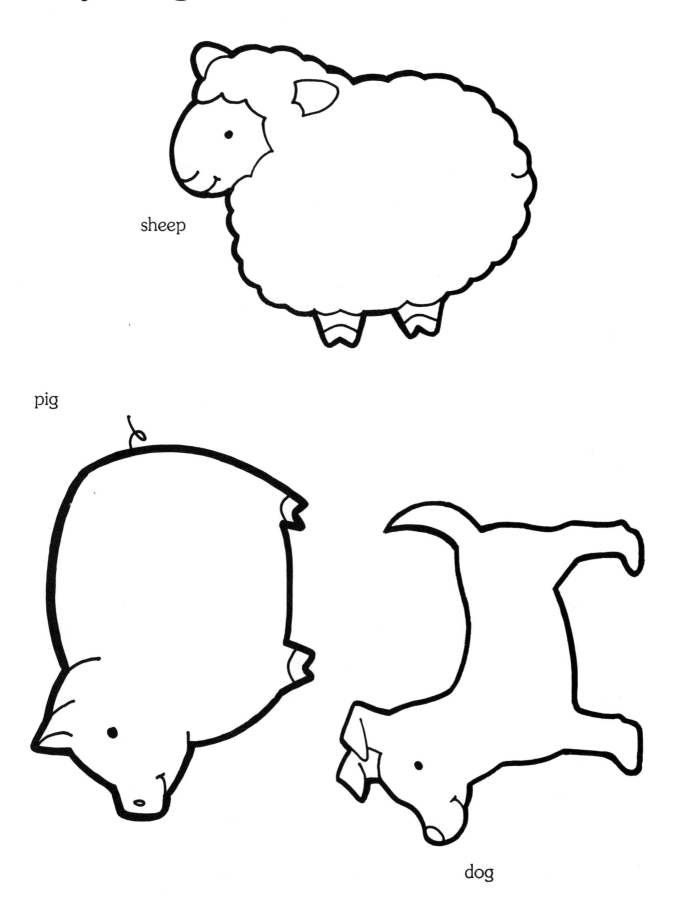

sheep

pig

dog

Storytelling Patterns

cat

hen

duck

goose

Storytelling Patterns

cow

horse

Storytelling Patterns

boy   grandmother

The Very Hungry Caterpillar

In this book, a caterpillar hatches from an egg. He is so hungry that each day of the week he eats his way through more and more food until he gets a stomachache. Then he eats a nice green leaf and feels better. Finally, he becomes a big, fat caterpillar and builds a cocoon around himself. Two weeks later, a beautiful butterfly emerges. The Very Hungry Caterpillar by Eric Carle (Philomel, 1969).

Related Books

The following books focus on insects, birth, and life cycles.

All Year Long by Nancy Tafuri (Greenwillow, 1983).

Backyard Insects by Millicent Selsam and Ronald Goor (Four Wings, 1983).

Discovering Butterflies by Douglas Florian (Scribner's, 1986).

A Duckling Is Born by Hans-Heinrich Isenbart (Putnam, 1981).

The Grouchy Ladybug by Eric Carle (Harper & Row, 1977).

An Insect's Body by Joanna Cole (Morrow, 1984).

A Kitten Is Born by Heiderose and Andreas Fischer-Nagel (Putnam, 1983).

Life of the Ladybug by Andreas and Heiderose Fischer-Nagel (Putnam, 1986).

La Oruga Muy Hambrienta (The Very Hungry Caterpillar, Spanish Language Edition) by Eric Carle (Philomel, 1969).

The Spit Bug Who Couldn't Spit by Penny Pollack (Putnam, 1982).

Cooking Activities

Butterfly Cookies

1 roll refrigerated cookie dough   5 oranges

1 can vanilla icing   raisins

Help the children slice the cookie dough and place the rounds on an ungreased cookie sheet. Bake at 375 degrees for nine to eleven minutes. Remove the cookies from the pan and cool. Help the children spread some icing on each cookie. Then slice the oranges and cut each slice in half. Help the children place a half-slice of orange on each side of a cookie for butterfly wings. Let the children put a raisin at the top of the cookie for the butterfly's head. Makes approximately 20 cookies.

Caterpillar Kabobs

a variety of fruit, depending on the season

Help the children cut the fruit into small cubes. Then let each child make a kabob by pushing several pieces of fruit onto a wooden skewer.

Art Activities

Paper Plate Caterpillars

Materials: 9" paper plates, green tempera paint, brushes, scissors, green pipe cleaners, brads, markers, tape

Preparation: Cut out the inner circles of enough paper plates to give one to each child. Cut each remaining rim into two pieces. Cut the pipe cleaners in half.

Activity: Have the children paint the paper plate centers and rims green. Let them use markers to draw caterpillar facial features on the center. Help the children tape a pipe cleaner piece to each side of the back of the center circle to form antennae. Fasten the two rim pieces together, one facing left and one facing right, with a brad to form the caterpillar's body. Help the children attach the caterpillar's head to the body with tape.

Butterfly Wings

Materials: construction paper, markers, tempera paint, plastic tub, newspaper

Preparation: Put some tempera paint in the tub. Draw a butterfly body—no wings—on a piece of construction paper for each child. Spread newspaper on the floor or the ground around the tub.

Activity: Place the first child's butterfly drawing on the newspaper next to the paint. Have the child dip a bare foot in the tempera paint, then make a footprint "wing" on one side of the butterfly's body. Have the child make another footprint on the other side of the butterfly for the other wing. Extra paint can be stamped off on the newspaper.

Coffee Filter Butterflies

Materials: coffee filters, black pipe cleaners, several colors of food coloring, eyedroppers, water, small bowls

Preparation: Mix three or four colors of food coloring and water in several bowls.

Activity: Have each child spread out a coffee filter so it's flat. Help the children pull up and pinch together their filter in the middle and secure it with a pipe cleaner. This forms the butterfly's body. Then show the children how to squeeze the eyedropper to pick up food coloring, then drop the coloring onto the filter edges. The colors will run together and create new colors. Let dry. Have the children spread out the butterflies.

Storytelling

Bookmaking

Materials: bookmaking patterns, green construction paper, lined or unlined writing paper, pipe cleaners, sequins, feathers, fabric or wrapping paper scraps, scissors, glue, tape, markers, stapler

Preparation: Duplicate enough caterpillar and antenna patterns on green construction paper so that each child gets two of each. Cut the patterns out, or let the children do the cutting if they are able. Duplicate the body pattern on writing paper (use the dotted line as a guide) so that each child receives three or four pieces.

Activity: Have each child decorate one of the green caterpillar shapes for the front of the book; sequins, feathers, fabric scraps, and so on can be glued on. Have the children glue each antenna circle to the end of a pipe cleaner. Then help the children tape the pipe cleaner antennae to the back of the caterpillar pattern. Let the children draw caterpillar facial features with markers. Next, help the children staple their caterpillar face to the writing paper and the other green pattern across the top, making a book. Let the children use the inside sections of the book for drawing, writing, or dictating. (See the completed book on the first page of this kit.)

Flannel Board Storytelling

Materials: storytelling patterns; green, red, brown, pink, yellow, white, purple, blue, and orange felt; tin foil; 2" Velcro strip; poster board; markers; glue; flannel board; scissors; craft knife

Preparation: Cut out the patterns. Trace each pattern except the moon on the appropriate color of felt. Cut out the felt patterns and add details with markers, glue, or additional pieces of felt. Trace the moon pattern on poster board. Cut out the pattern and cover it with tin foil. Glue the Velcro strip to the back of the moon to hold it on the flannel board. Put the food patterns in the order in which they're mentioned in the story.

Activity: Place the moon and the green leaf on the flannel board. Then begin to read or retell the story. Put the egg pattern on as you read or tell the first page. Remove all the patterns. Place the sun and the little caterpillar on as you tell the second page. Leave the sun on the board as you tell what the caterpillar ate, adding the food patterns in order, then removing them. Then remove the sun and the little caterpillar. Add, then remove the big caterpillar. Fold the butterfly and place it behind the cocoon; put both pieces on the board. Remove the cocoon and open the butterfly as you read the last page.

To extend the storytelling, you may want to take the children on a walk to look for different leaf shapes and types. Leaves could also be collected and used to make crayon rubbings to display with the Paper Plate Caterpillars.

Bookmaking Patterns

antenna

body

antenna

Storytelling Patterns

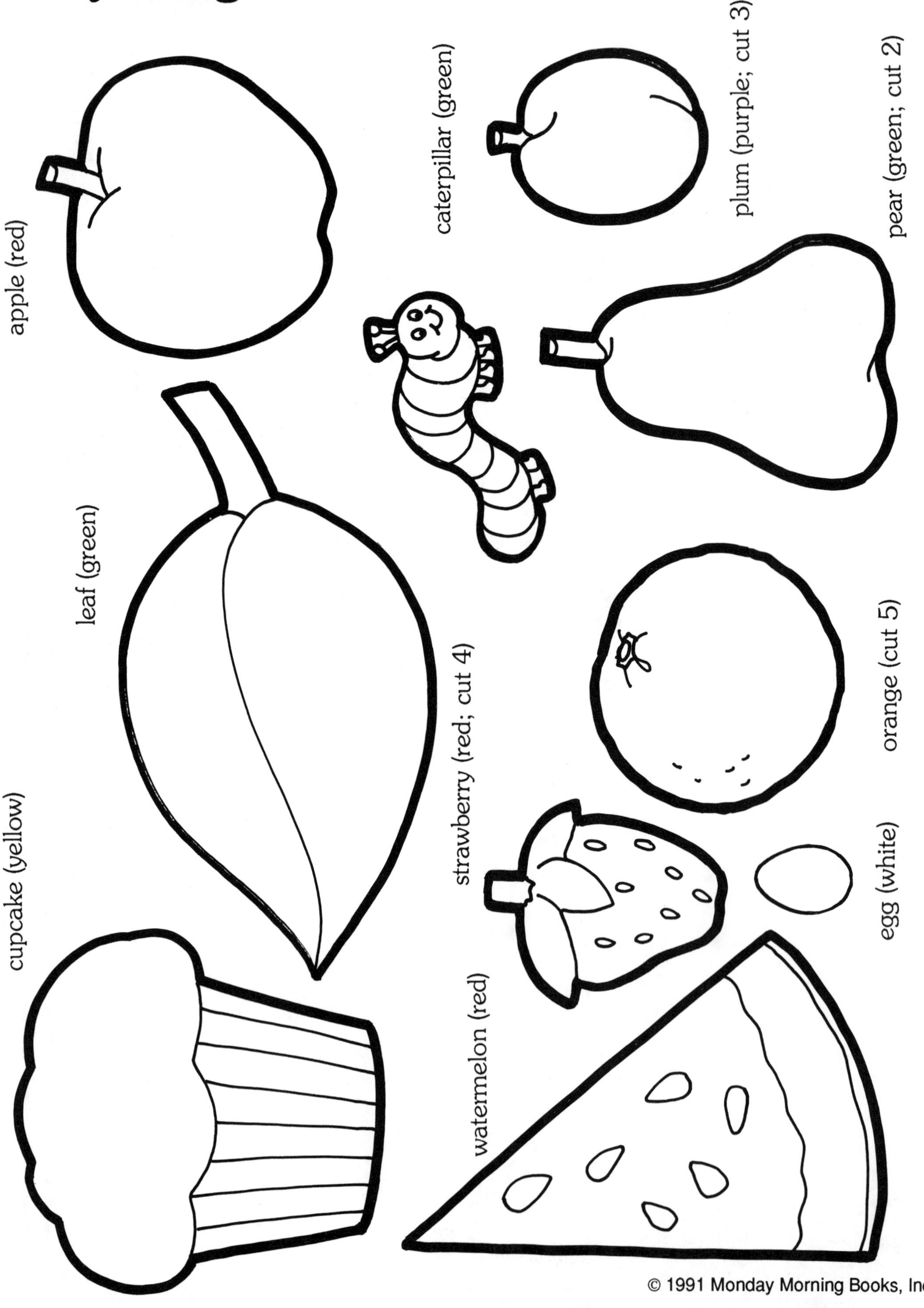

apple (red)

caterpillar (green)

plum (purple; cut 3)

pear (green; cut 2)

leaf (green)

strawberry (red; cut 4)

orange (cut 5)

cupcake (yellow)

watermelon (red)

egg (white)

Storytelling Patterns

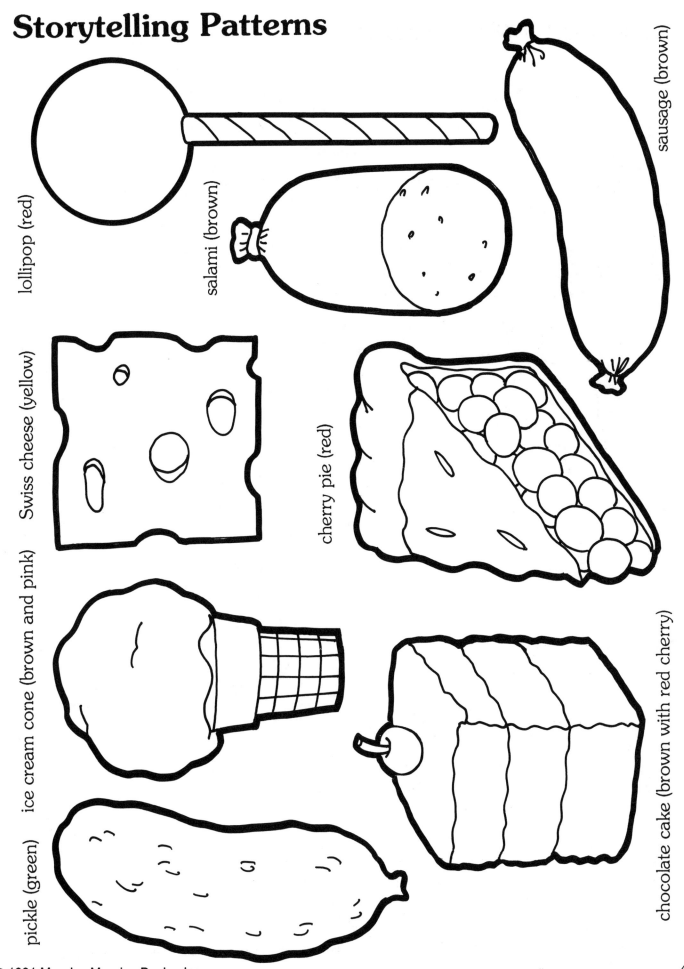

lollipop (red)

sausage (brown)

salami (brown)

Swiss cheese (yellow)

cherry pie (red)

ice cream cone (brown and pink)

chocolate cake (brown with red cherry)

pickle (green)

Storytelling Patterns

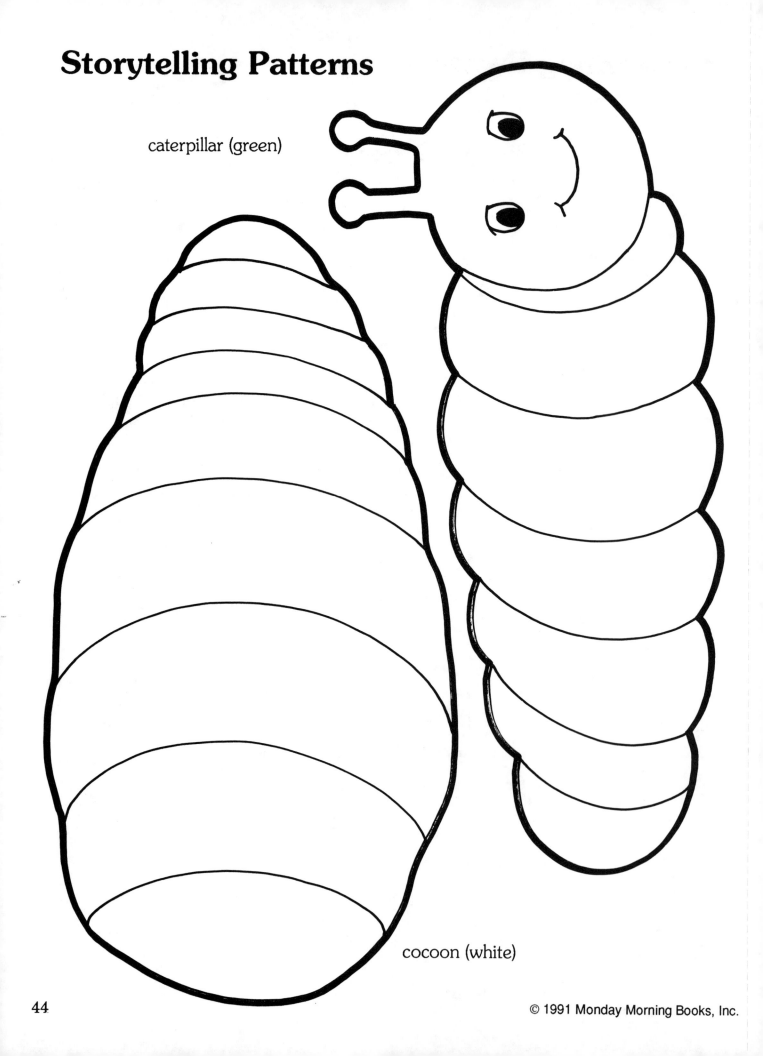

caterpillar (green)

cocoon (white)

Storytelling Patterns

butterfly (orange)

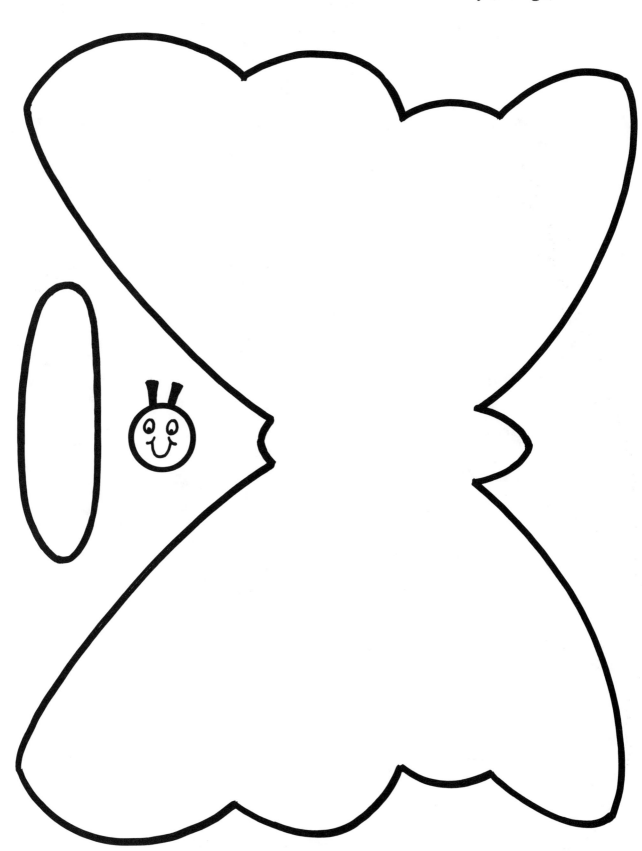

45

Storytelling Patterns

sun (yellow)

moon (silver)

The Mitten

The Mitten, an old Ukranian cumulative folk tale, tells the story of a young boy who loses one of his mittens while gathering wood in the forest. A mouse finds the mitten and uses it as shelter from the cold. Then the mouse allows a series of animals to share his shelter until the mitten is so full it bursts, popping the animals back into the snow. When the little boy returns to find his mitten, he sees it is destroyed, and his grandmother knits him a new pair. The Mitten by Alvin Tresselt (Lothrop, 1964).

Related Books

The following books feature winter, snow, grandparents, homes, and mittens.

Anna, Grandpa, and the Big Storm by Carla Stevens (Puffin, 1986).

Beneath a Blue Umbrella by Jack Prelutsky (Greenwillow, 1990).

Grandma's Promise by Elaine Moore (Lothrop, 1988).

A House Is a House for Me by Mary Ann Hoberman (Viking, 1985).

The Mystery of the Missing Red Mitten by Steven Kellogg (Dial, 1974).

Runaway Mittens by Jean Rogers (Greenwillow, 1988).

Snow Woman by David McKee (Lothrop, 1988).

The Snowy Day by Ezra Jack Keats (Viking, 1962).

Stopping by the Woods on a Snowy Evening by Robert Frost (Dutton, 1978).

The Three Little Kittens by Lorinda Cauley (Putnam, 1982).

Winter Barn by Peter Parnall (Macmillan, 1986).

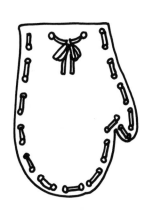

Cooking Activities

Snowballs

$\frac{3}{4}$ cup marshmallow cream   2 cups peanut butter

3 ounces chocolate chips   shredded coconut

Have the children mix everything but the coconut in a large bowl. Help the children roll the mixture into balls. Then let the children roll the balls in the coconut. Refrigerate. Serves 25 children.

Mittens in the Snow

1 large graham cracker per child   raisins

soft cream cheese

Have the children spread the softened cream cheese on the graham crackers. Let them outline a mitten shape on each cracker with raisins.

Hot Chocolate

1 25-ounce package dry milk   2 cups powdered sugar

1 jar nondairy creamer   1 16-ounce can powdered chocolate

boiling water

Mix all the ingredients together. For each serving, mix three tablespoons of the mixture with boiling water; be sure an adult pours the water. Stir well. Makes 100 servings.

Art Activities

Whipped Snow Paintings

Materials: 1 cup Ivory Snow flakes, dark construction paper, paintbrushes, eggbeater, large bowl containing $\frac{1}{2}$ cup warm water

Preparation: Use the eggbeater to beat the cup of flakes into the water. Beat until frothy.

Activity: Have the children paint the white flakes onto the dark construction paper.

Spatter Paint Snowflakes

Materials: white construction paper, scissors, toothbrushes, blue tempera paint, water, bowls

Preparation: Cut enough different snowflake patterns from construction paper to give one to each child. Add water to the tempera to thin it.

Activity: Have each child place a snowflake pattern on a piece of white construction paper. Let the children dip their toothbrushes in the paint mixture, point the bristles at their paper, and run their fingers across the bristles to make the paint spatter over the construction paper (it will also spatter on the snowflake pattern). Encourage the children to spatter the paint thickly. When each pattern is removed, a white snowflake will be outlined in a blue sky.

Tracks in the Snow

Materials: sponges, scissors, white construction paper, brown or black tempera paint, bowls

Preparation: Cut several different animal footprint shapes from the sponges. Distribute a sheet of construction paper to each child.

Activity: Have each child dip a footprint-shaped sponge into the dark paint and make animal tracks with it on the paper— the snow.

Storytelling

Bookmaking

Materials: bookmaking pattern, assorted colors of construction paper, scissors, lined or unlined writing paper, markers, ribbon, fabric scraps, yarn, hole punch, blunt needles, glue

Preparation: Duplicate enough patterns on construction paper so that each child will have two. Cut out the shapes using the solid lines as your guide, or let the children do the cutting. Punch two holes in all the shapes as indicated on the pattern. Then punch holes around the outside edge of half the mitten shapes and give each child one punched mitten and one unpunched mitten. Duplicate enough patterns on writing paper (use the dotted line as a guide) so that each child will have three or four pieces. Cut out the patterns and punch two holes in them as indicated. Thread the needles with yarn.

Activity: Have the children sew around the edge of the hole-punched pattern with yarn, then decorate this book cover with fabric scraps, ribbon, and yarn. Help the children assemble their books, putting the paper between the covers. Help them thread ribbon through the two holes and tie the book together. Encourage the children to use the books for writing, drawing, and dictating. (See the completed book on the first page of the chapter.)

Pocket Storytelling

Materials: storytelling patterns, assorted colors of construction paper, scissors, markers, felt, lace, yarn, fabric scraps, glue, laminating film or clear Contact paper, needle and thread

Preparation: Make the mitten pocket by tracing the tip of the mitten (the dotted line) on felt, then turning the pattern and tracing the thumb portion (the solid line) below it. Cut out two of these large mitten shapes and sew them together to form a large mitten pocket. Glue lace, yarn, and fabric scraps to the mitten. To make the pocket props, trace each animal pattern on the appropriate color of construction paper. Cut the patterns out. Use the markers to add detail. Laminate the shapes or cover them with clear Contact paper.

Activity: Place the pocket props face down in the order in which they appear in the story. Hold the mitten pocket in your lap. As you read or retell the story, place the animals into the mitten. At the appropriate time, turn the mitten upside down and shake all the animals out onto the floor or your lap. Encourage the children to retell the story, placing the animals in the pocket. Also discuss with them some of their own experiences in which they shared a warm place with or gave help to a friend.

Bookmaking Pattern

Storytelling Pattern: Mitten Pocket

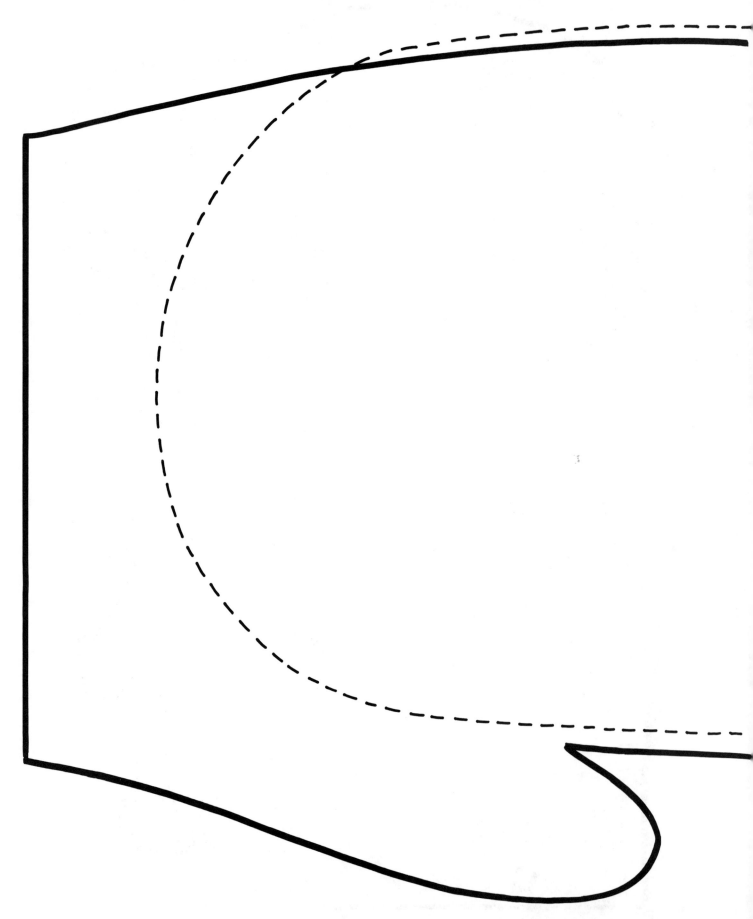

Storytelling Patterns

mouse

frog

owl

rabbit

Storytelling Patterns

wolf

fox

Storytelling Patterns

boar

cricket

Storytelling Pattern

bear

Mr. Gumpy's Outing

This repetitive tale tells of a series of animals and children who ask to take a ride in Mr. Gumpy's boat. Mr. Gumpy kindly allows two children and one goat, calf, chicken, sheep, pig, dog, cat, and rabbit to climb aboard with him. He warns each passenger not to make a fuss. Everyone quietly agrees, but suddenly, when they're all on the boat, they make a terrible fuss. The boat tips over and everyone falls into the water. Mr. Gumpy invites them all to his home for tea. <u>Mr. Gumpy's Outing</u> by John Burningham (Holt, 1978).

Related Books

The following books focus on boats, animal sounds, and one too many in a small space.

<u>Animal Sounds</u> by Aurelius Battaglia (Western, 1981).

<u>Boat Book</u> by Gail Gibbons (Holiday House, 1983).

<u>Boats</u> by Anne Rockwell (Dutton, 1982).

<u>Euphonia and the Flood</u> by Mary Calhoun (Parents' Magazine Press, 1976).

<u>Gobble, Growl, Grunt</u> by Peter Spier (Doubleday, 1988).

<u>Mr. Gumpy's Motor Car</u> by John Burningham (Crowell, 1973).

<u>Mushroom in the Rain</u> by Mirra Ginsburg (Macmillan, 1974).

<u>"Quack," Said the Billy Goat</u> by Charles Causley (Lippincott, 1986).

<u>Thidwick the Big Hearted Moose</u> by Dr. Seuss (Random House, 1948).

<u>Who Sank the Boat?</u> by Pamela Allen (Coward, 1983).

Cooking Activities

Tea Biscuits

$\frac{1}{2}$ cup margarine

$\frac{1}{2}$ cup sugar

1 teaspoon finely shredded lemon peel

1 egg

2 tablespoons lemon juice

$1\frac{1}{4}$ cup all-purpose flour

$\frac{1}{2}$ teaspoon baking powder

$\frac{1}{4}$ teaspoon salt

$\frac{1}{2}$ cup raisins

Preheat the oven to 375 degrees. Then let the children do the following steps: Beat the margarine in a large bowl until softened; add the sugar and lemon peel and beat again until fluffy; add the egg and the lemon juice and beat well. In another bowl, have the children mix the flour, baking powder, and salt. Then have them gradually add the flour mixture to the butter mixture and beat until well mixed. Finally, have the children stir in the raisins. Ask the children to drop the mixture by teaspoonfuls onto ungreased cookie sheets. Bake at 375 degrees for eight to ten minutes. Serves 30 children.

Spiced Tea

1 11-ounce jar Tang

2 3-ounce packages sweetened lemonade mix

1 cup instant tea

boiling water

1 cup sugar

$\frac{1}{2}$ teaspoon cinnamon

$\frac{1}{2}$ teaspoon cloves

Have the children combine all the ingredients in a large bowl. For each serving, let the children spoon three teaspoons of the mixture into a cup, add boiling water (be sure an adult pours the water), and stir well. Serves 75.

River Mud Candy

1 stick margarine

$\frac{1}{2}$ cup milk

2 cups sugar

$\frac{1}{4}$ cup cocoa

3 heaping teaspoons peanut butter

$2\frac{1}{2}$ cups uncooked oatmeal

Have the children combine the margarine, milk, and sugar in a large pan. Bring the mixture to a boil. Have the children add the cocoa and the peanut butter. Continue boiling for three to five minutes, supervising the children as they continuously stir the mixture. Remove the pan from the heat. Have the children add the oatmeal. Then let them drop the mixture by teaspoonfuls onto wax paper. Cool. Serves 30 children.

Art Activities

Raging River

Materials: large sheet of butcher paper, Styrofoam cups, several colors of tempera paint, large needle

Preparation: Use the needle to punch a single hole in the bottom of each Styrofoam cup. Pour a little paint into each cup just before the children begin to do their artwork.

Activity: Encourage the children to move the cups over a large sheet of butcher paper to jointly create a raging river. The paint will dribble out slowly or quickly depending on the size of the hole. Encourage each child to use several colors of paint.

Chalk Boats

Materials: white construction paper, wet sponge, colored chalk, scissors

Preparation: Cut the paper into different-shaped boats (rowboats, battleships, sailboats, etc.). Wet the paper slightly with the sponge.

Activity: Have the children draw on the boats with the colored chalk, making whatever designs they like. Encourage the children to use the sides as well as the ends of the chalk for different results.

Sandpaper Prints

Materials: medium-grade sandpaper, wax crayons, white paper, iron

Activity: Have the children use the wax crayons to draw a picture of Mr. Gumpy, his boat, or one of the animals on the boat on the sandpaper. Place each sandpaper drawing, drawing side down, on a piece of white paper. Press the warm iron over the drawing. Lift off the sandpaper to view the print.

Storytelling

Bookmaking

Materials: bookmaking pattern, tagboard, markers, construction paper, lined or unlined writing paper, scissors, stapler

Preparation: Duplicate the pattern of Mr. Gumpy and his boat onto tagboard so that each child receives one. Cut the patterns out, or let the children do the cutting. Duplicate just the boat part of the pattern onto construction paper so that each child receives one. Cut the patterns out. Then duplicate the boat part of the pattern again on the writing paper; cut out enough patterns on the dotted lines so that each child receives three or four sheets.

Activity: Let the children use the markers to color Mr. Gumpy and his boat. Help the children assemble their books by using the tagboard boat with Mr. Gumpy as the back cover, the construction paper boat as the front cover, and putting the writing paper in between. Staple the book together as indicated on the pattern. Encourage the children to use their books for writing, drawing, or dictating about other possible passengers in Mr. Gumpy's boat. They could also make up a story about another journey in Mr. Gumpy's boat. (See the completed book on the first page of this kit.)

Object Storytelling

Materials: storytelling patterns, 14" x 10" cardboard box; small cardboard box or paper bag; 12 6-inch cardboard tubes; glue; scissors; pink, white, black, brown, yellow, orange, and gray tempera paint and construction paper; brushes; laminating film or clear Contact paper; markers

Preparation: Duplicate the patterns of the people's and animals' heads onto assorted colors of construction paper as indicated. Add details with markers. Laminate or cover the shapes with laminating film or clear Contact paper. Paint the tubes to match the characters. Glue the heads to the tubes. Then duplicate the boat patterns on brown construction paper. Add details with markers. Laminate the boats or cover them with clear Contact paper. Glue one boat to each side of the larger box.

Activity: Begin by placing the empty cardboard box with the boats glued to it on a table next to you. Place the characters in the small box or bag. As you read or tell the story, place each character in the boat box. Knock the boat over at the appropriate time. Then line the characters up on the table when the story ends and everyone follows Mr. Gumpy to his house for tea. After the children have heard and retold the story, encourage them to discuss the story's theme and the characters' relationships. Then you may want to compare the story with another story such as <u>The Mitten</u> or <u>Cat Goes Fiddle-i-fee</u>.

Bookmaking Pattern

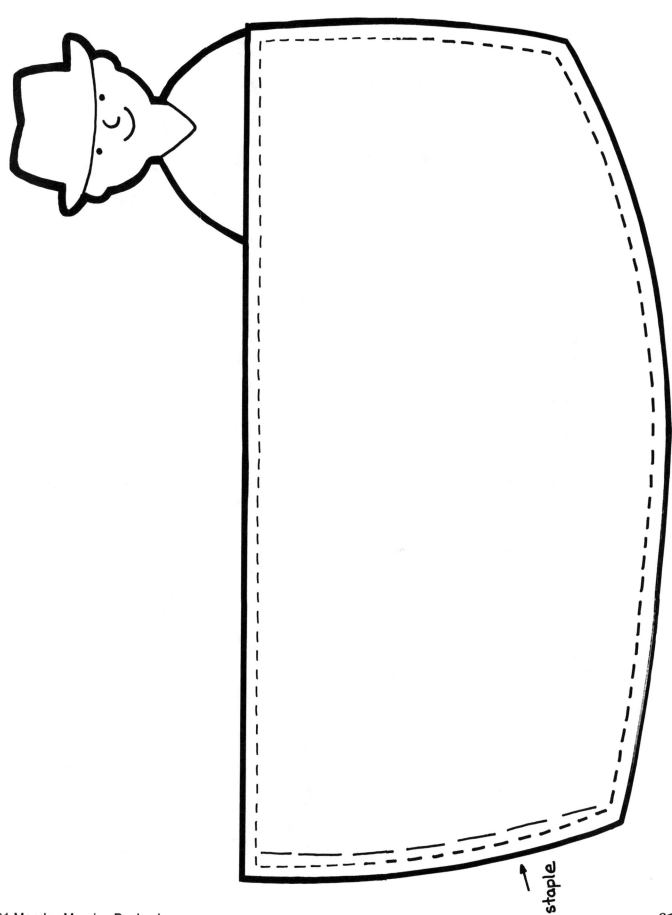

staple

Storytelling Patterns

rabbit (pink)

Mr. Gumpy
(any appropriate color)

boy
(any appropriate color)

cat (gray)

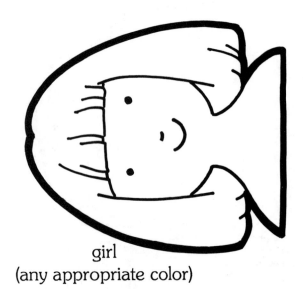

girl
(any appropriate color)

dog (brown)

Storytelling Patterns

cow (brown)

pig (pink)

chicken (yellow)

rooster (orange)

goat (white)

sheep (white)

Storytelling Pattern: Boat (brown)

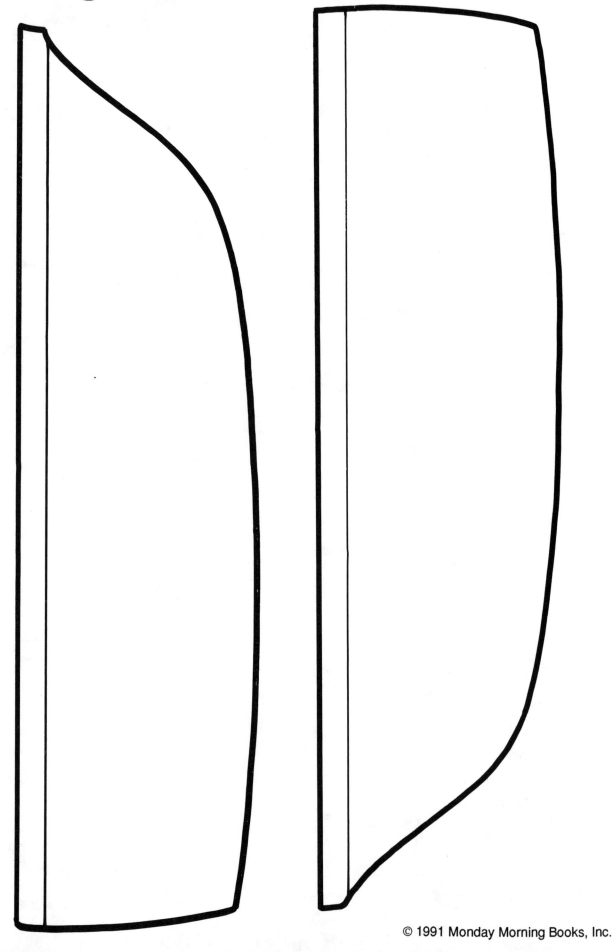